Something For You

A Collection of Short Stories & Poems

Something For You

A Collection of Short Stories & Poems

Written by
Walena Mayson

Paperback ISBN: 979-8-9865891-7-6

10 9 8 7 6 5 4 3 2 1

Note:

The publisher is not responsible for the content of this book nor websites, or social media pages (or their content).

Dedication

First, I would like to thank my Heavenly Father and my Earthly father for loving me unconditionally. I remember growing up... My earthly father name Walter Edward Moss would always tell me if you find your passion you'll never work hard again.

Oh, daddy you were so cautious in this pandemic so when you lost your battle to the Covid-19 on February 25, 2021 I was\am so devastated! I wish you would've let me make it up to you. I wanted to be your caregiver, you were my best friend, my hero, my dad. You were my spiritual advisor, favorite comedian and my heaven on earth...

I couldn't do no wrong in your eyes! I was your spoiled brat! Thank you for always having my back even when I felt like the world was against me! Yes, indeed when my last day come on earth I'm running to your loving arms! Me, Nene and Toya miss you dearly!

Walter "Tee – Lee" Edward Moss

Tell God You're Thankful For Everything You Have In This Life

1. Your eyes
2. Your nose
3. Your arms
4. Your legs
5. Your feet
6. Your liver
7. Your kidneys
8. Your heart
9. Your mind
10. Your soul
11. Your family
12. Your house
13. Your kids
14. Your vehicle (car/truck/van)
15. Your career or job
16. Your sisters
17. Your brothers
18. Your personality
19. Your wealth
20. Your health
21. Your life
22. Your life partner
23. Your friends
24. Your neighborhood
25. Your church

26. Your doctor
27. Your teachers
28. Your haters (because they know you're somebody)
29. Most of all I'm thankful for your unconditional love Lord of God.

My Love Question

1.   Do you love God?
2.   How is your relationship with God?
3.   Are you afraid of dying?
4.   What are your hobbies?
5.   What are your bad habits?
6.   Are you addicted to pornography?
7.   How do you show affection?
8.   Do you want to get married?
9.   If so, would you go see a marriage counselor?
10. How many times a week do you think a woman should cook?
11. Would you date a woman who couldn't cook?
12. Do you know how to cook? If so, would you help out?
13. Do you believe every man should work to provide for his home to be the leader? The king?
14. Do you believe only the man to take out the trash or do outside jobs like cutting the grass?

15. How important is education for you?

16. Are you controlling?

17. Have you ever abused someone?

18. Would you date a woman with an in curable disease such as Ebola, cancer, lupus, diabetes, HIV, herpes, blindness, and missing arms or legs?

19. Do you have any illness?

20. Do you exercise?

21. Do you eat healthy?

22. Do you have children?

23. If you don't have any, do you want any?

24. Are you good with saving money?

25. Do you have any dreams or goals you would like to start?

26. Do you believe your spouse should be your best friend?

27. Do you like to travel?

28. Are you close with your family?

29. Would you go to the store to buy tampons and pads for your woman?

30. Are you willing to pray with your spouse every morning?

31. Do you have any hidden talents?

32. Have you ever been arrested?

33. Have you ever killed someone? Even if it
    was self-defense?
34. Do you have bad credit? Or a good
    credit?
35. Do you believe you should go half on
    the bills with your spouse?
36. How often do you need sex in your
    relationship?
37. Do you like oral sex?
38. Would you go to church with me?

I've written this questionnaire for my future
husband to see if we're compatible so we
could exist without conflict and to see what
we expect from each other and our thoughts
about life. This questionnaire can also be
used for reevaluating your relationship and
in your marriage right. Use the questions to
look in the mirror from time to time.

Your Life Mission

- On this earth our mission should be to die empty!
- Serve the Lord with gladness! Be an excellent servant.
- Write all the books your hands will allow for the Lord.
- If you're a singer, sing as many songs as your vocal cord will allow for the Lord.
- Feed the homeless, the less fortunate and animals.
- Let your behavior and thought match God Word!
- Daily in prayer, ask God to touch your heart and mind.
- Invent something that others can apply to their lives.
- Grow closer to family and friends.
- Contribute to the earth by planting trees, flowers, reproduce great kids, and give off positive energy.
- Give back to nature by feeding ducks, cats, dogs, birds, fishes and turtles.

Commander in Chief
(President of the United States)

* As a community, nation and region we need a president who cares about local and international affairs.
* Someone who will make house calls with print money to help all families across America.
* Someone who will give black families 1 acre and a mule.
* Someone who is not racist.
* Someone who have experience in Air Force, Navy or the Army.
* Someone who served as a Senator or a Mayor.
* Someone who is spiritual with knowledge and wisdom.
* Someone who will give our world peace on earth.
* Someone who will support small business owners.
* Someone who will grant us income tax refunds every month.

Hey Unknown Queen

Long time no see, you know the crazy thing about it… I feel like I'm a reflection of you. You're so beautiful, godly and always giving God praise through your trials and storms. You always trust in the Lord and you're a peaceful person. I feel like you have a heart of gold. I'm thankful to call you, my friend. We might not see each other every day but you can bet your last dollar I'm a phone call away.

I will always be there with you in spirit. Whether you want to talk about relationships, family, God or life problems. I am a shoulder to lean on, a hand to hold and ear to hear about whatever you're going through. I know we have a special connection. You're one of my angels walking this earth. You give me hope for tomorrow! Please remember to celebrate your life every day and have fun.

People That Influenced Me

1. My Heavenly Father Jesus Christ
2. Walter Moss – my Earthly father
3. Latonya Moss - my earthly mother
4. Latoya Moss - my baby sister and best friend
5. Janitha Wheat - my older sister and best friend
6. Shakira Standifer - my only child/daughter/best friend
7. Nellie Moss - my grandmother
8. Pastor Troy and 2 Pac
9. Fox - my favorite uncle
10. Roy Lee - my uncle
11. Janice Moss – my auntie
12. Dexter Moss - my uncle
13. Uncle Moonie & Auntie Marsha
14. Past lovers I had? Lol
15. Adina Howard music
16. Patrice Rushen music
17. Alexander O'Neal music
18. Denise Austin workout tapes
19. Eddie Murphy stand ups/movies

20. Chris Rock stand ups/movies
21. Monifah music
22. Ice Cube music/movies
23. Ira Burton my great-grandfather & Johnny Lee Moss (Pop)
24. The Gap Band music
25. Morris Day and The Time music
26. Janaya Harvey
27. Big cousin/Big Brother Melvin
28. Auntie Miranda &cousin Donald
29. Different every day strangers I meet at stores, restaurants, movie theaters, gym, etc.
30. Mokesha - my cousin
31. Shante - my cousin
32. Muffin - my cousin
33. Uncle Nate & Auntie Darryell
34. Catherine Moss
35. Rebecca Moss
36. Jessica Moss

How Could You

When I met you, I thought you were my prince charming. I was walking down the street heading to the library with my daughter. It was a very hot summer day; I look at you with your muscles bursting out of your colorful tank top. My first impression of you was… I thought you were sexy, but I could see the lust in your eyes.

So, we got in your green Scooby Doo van and we started chatting a little… Both of us had strong personalities but it was a turn on. Then before dropping us off, you asked for my telephone number so I put my name and number in your phone and I told you I will call you when I get home.

Two hours later once I got back home, I called you and you asked me could I have company. I said sure because I wanted to be close to you. So, we spent all day and night together and we were inseparable for the next seven years on and off. It was so easy to talk with you, because you were a homebody like me but sometimes you were creep off.

We had built a great friendship. I always felt so comfortable with you I really trusted you. Legally you were already married but you have been separated before I even met you. We would have sex every day I always used to tell you please don't do anything that will separate us. Five years into our relationship you proposed to me.

I was so happy plus we were living together. The only thing about our relationship I felt was very controlling, are the times that you asked who I hung around and the places I would go. We only got into one physical altercation which in my past I've been in several. At times I would break up with you because I noticed you were a ladies' man, a cheater and a thief.

I remember one time inviting you to my old church and you brought snacks and started eating in there. Then you had the nerve to tell me one of the girls in the church choir was pretty and she reminded you of one of your daughters. I heard God tell me then to leave but I just didn't want to be alone. Then a week later your daughter accused you of touching her. I didn't want to believe that you would stoop so low.

You even came to my job crying and pleading telling me you were innocent I thought I knew you. Then the next day I heard you was charged for this crime. You came over to a mutual friend house of ours asking for something to eat and trying to tell us everybody was lying on you. The next thing I knew the police officers and news reporters were kicking down the door. I gave a statement hiding my face because I didn't want no involvement. How could I love go so wrong?

You left me lonely, sad, confused and hurt but the grace of God I got through it. I forgive you! I pray you receive the help you need I know you shared with me how you had a horrible childhood. But you have to deal with the pain and correct your actions through healing.

If Jesus Was My Husband

My house and land would be FREE (paid by his blood)! I could travel around the world anytime with my angel wings. He would own my heart.

When we make love, it would feel like Heaven (we would feel like every day is our holiday honeymoon and it will feel like our first sexual encounter each time).

As a housewife I will keep the house warm with my heart. Every day when I look into his eyes, I would have tears of joy. He would be a jack of all trades and never be mean to me. He would love me to give him pleasure by licking,touching,grabbing and kissing all over Him until the end of times.

We will never have an Easter crucifixion day!

I Never Thought

I Never thought I'll be alone.

Never Thought I'll have a house to call my home.

Never thought I'll need a friend.

Never thought I'll be unhappy again.

Never thought I'll have to work so much.

Never thought I'll have a relationship that will last.

Never thought I'll be broke again.

Never thought I'll be so sad.

Never thought I'll be so mad.

Never thought that it would hurt so much, I can really feel it in my gut.

Never thought I would trust again.

Never thought things would turn around.

I really hope I will never have to say never again!

Falling In Love

The feeling of butterflies in my stomach.
Seeing stars in your eyes.

Feeling fireworks between my legs. My heart
skips a beat every time you're around me.
You take my loneliness away.

I have a song singing inside of my heart.

I feel dizzy looking into your puppy dog
eyes.

I want to travel the world with you and taste
different foods.

I desire to be a better person.

I feel safe and secure with you.

I feel a natural high.

I feel a rush.

I'm overwhelmed with joy.

Words to Describe Me

1. Mother
2. Daughter
3. Sister
4. Niece
5. Cousin
6. Friend
7. Workaholic
8. Funny
9. Loveable
10. Overweighed
11. Sexy
12. Spontaneous
13. Brave
14. Outspoken
15. Loud
16. Caring
17. Spiritual Vessel
18. Cooker
19. Cleaner
20. Head Hunter
21. Strong-minded
22. Leader
23. Ambitious

24. Lover

25. Storyteller

26. Supporter

27. Aggressive

28. Shy

29. Friendly

30. Mean

31. Silly

32. Crazy

33. Wild

34. Fun

35. Private

36. Graceful

37. Faithful

38. Loyal

39. Honest

40. Peaceful

41. Free

42. Knowledgeable

43. Wise

44. Understanding

45. Determined

46. Charming

47. Prayer Warrior

I Just Want To Be Happy

- Care-Free
- Stress-Free
- Drama-Free
- Fly high like a bird or a plane.
- I don't want this crazy world to drive me insane.
- I desire a lover that will rub my feet and shoulder.
- Deep inside of my soul, I want to travel the world.
- Help the less fortunate.
- Be grateful for every breath.
- No longer will I hold onto people or things that hurt me.

How To Deal With Being Alone On The Holidays

1. When you first wake up and pray and meditate ask God to clear your mind so you can hear a positive word from him.
2. Breathe and relax.
3. Go treat yourself to a meal.
4. Go to church.
5. Take a drive.
6. Listen to music.
7. Go watch a movie at your local theater.
8. Remember you're alone because maybe you left a bad relationship or the person left because they didn't deserve you!
9. Go work out.
10. Go shopping for yourself.
11. Build your confidence level up.
12. Go do some volunteer work.
13. And if all else fails… pray some more.

My Perfect Man

- Godly (chasing God own heart).
- Hard Worker
- Honest
- Faithful
- Loyal
- Great Father
- Great Lover
- Sexy with Muscles
- Who only have eyes for me.
- Who's nice to me and my family.
- Who enjoys feeding birds, ducks and taking walks and watching the stars at night.
- Who won't abuse me mentally, sexually, physically or emotionally.
- He's a great leader and give good advice.
- Who serves his community with his heart and not his penis.

My Christmas Wish List

- Inner Peace
- Peace on Earth
- God send my husband that's personalized for me.
- I hit my weight goal of 150 pounds.
- My daughter, Shakira deserves everything wants for Christmas.
- God heals my sisters.
- God heals my father and mother.
- God let me hit the Powerball.
- I buy my 1st house.
- I print my 1st book.
- Get a new paint job on my car.
- I spread a lot of Christmas cheer (passing out hugs, kisses and ministering to others about Our Savior Jesus Christ).

Praying For a Husband 2022

I burst out in tears in prayer, as a single 38-year-old Christian woman because lately I've been feeling like I'll never be wed. But in the name of Jesus, I pray God protect my future husband. I pray he sees me as Rebecca in the Bible. A simple servant whom chasing after God own heart and who just want to be loved by a man of God! Lord, do a new thing in the midst of my tears! I get so tired of being lonely, struggling on my own and dating bad boys who just want to waste my time.

Falling for men who don't see the beauty inside of me. Lord, I pray he's not a killer, child molester, Womanizer, or fake husband. I want the real deal Holy Filled. Someone who can look past my ways and flaws or the material stuff I lack. He won't judge me based on my address, my car, my job, my book, my hairstyle, my nose ring or the funds I lack. He just sees my heart, Lord. Lord, let your will be done in my life.

My Homeless Testimony

In the summer of 2011, I was homeless. I slept in my Buick rendezvous' truck about 5 to 7 times, in between when I couldn't afford a hotel. What calls me to experience homelessness? I got out of a domestic violence situation and since the place was in his name, I had to leave. I only took my truck and clothes.... everything else I left behind. I know how it feels to work on a job and no one knows you're having a rough time!

Crashing over friends, family members and enemies' houses so I can stay warm through the night time. What a mighty God we serve. At the time, I had a small daughter so I let her go stay with her father for the summer. I didn't want my daughter to see me struggling financially. I feel anyone pain who is dealing with this!!!

Believe me joy comes in the morning! Remember Jesus loves you and as well as myself! My advice is, don't have too much pride! Let someone pass a blessing and help you.

Love always, Sister Mayson

I Want To Have More

1. More Happiness
2. More Peace
3. More Love
4. More Lovemaking
5. More Money in the Bank
6. More Homes
7. More Wigs
8. More of God
9. More Soul
10. More Desserts
11. More Beer
12. More Wine
13. More Fun
14. More Bowling
15. More Traveling
16. More Listening
17. More Achievements
18. More Goals
19. More Cars & Trucks
20. More Reading
21. More Praying to God
22. More Laughing
23. More Smiling

24. More Hugging
25. More Kissing
26. More Studying
27. More Excitement
28. More Kindness
29.Just more than enough for me!!!

He's Not Looking At That

1. Your eyes because they are sexy and slanted.
2. Your hair because it's a weave.
3. Your nose ring because it looks exotic.
4. Your teeth because you have a gap.
5. Your lips because you give great oral se
6. Your nipples because they stay hard like the room temperature is cold.
7. Your stomach because you have a muffin top.
8. Your thighs because you look like a mermaid.
9. Your legs because they look like chicken legs.
10. Your feet because he can see the corn through your shoes.

He just sees your heart, because you are chasing God!

A Day In My Life
(Wednesday 12/28/2016)

Woke up this morning at 5:30 AM. It's normal because I usually have to be at work at 6:30 AM. Monday through Friday for eight hours a day but I'm actually on vacation for the holidays, my vacation started December 23, 2016. But I'm flat broke and couldn't afford to go out of town or anything really, I haven't felt comfortable leaving my apartment since my place got broken into on November 19, 2016.

Lord, I'm praying I can get an alarm system so I can stop walking back-and-forth through my apartment. Like, now it's 7:44 PM and I'm looking out of my daughter's bedroom window and walking in my living room looking out of the windows also… feeling like a security guard wishing I had some groceries but I won't have any money until tomorrow when I get my child support. Maybe I'll treat myself to some ice cream because heaven knows I only ate one by Georgia boy sausage with a slice of bread and 3 cups of sweet tea and two bottles of water. I tell you the struggle is very real.

Then, I don't have cable plus my daughter is spending the holidays with her father so I'm kind of lonely. I wish my period wasn't on, so I could call back/text my lover but it's a blessing because I'm tired of feeling like a piece of meat… Hold on, I just ran to the window in my daughter's bedroom to see this black Honda that I heard was involved with my break in. I swear I wish I had some money saved so I could move. You know it's a difference between African-Americans – Black people – and dirty ass niggas who don't want to work. Only want to have sex with any and everybody, lie, cheat, steal, kill, gamble, drink and do all types of drugs and sell their food stamps while their kids are hungry. Abuse their lovers, parents or anyone who tells them the right path to go down. I tell you; this is hell on earth.

How To Be a Proverb 31 Woman

Who so find a wife find a good thing, and obtained favor of the Lord. House and riches are the inheritance of the fathers: and prudent wife is from the Lord. So, who can find a virtuous woman? For her price is far above rubies. The heart of her husband does it safely trust in her, so that he stole have no need to borrow. She will do him good and not evil all the days of her life. She is like the merchant ships; she brings food from afar. She stretches out her hand to the poor; yay she reached for her hands to the needy. She opens her mouth with wisdom; and in her tongue is a lot of kindness.

Her children arise up, and call her blessed; husband do too, and he praises her. A 2022 virtuous woman spend less time on social media worrying about who shot John. Let's finish this race ladies.

Work on your mind, body, spirit and soul. First don't use profanity against anyone – man, woman or child. Keep your body covered! Your body is a temple! Meditate and pray to God daily. Exercise daily – using treadmill, dumbbells, do some sit ups and push-ups. Listen to a gospel song every morning when you wake up! In the evening while cleaning your house listen to some R&B old-school music. Cook a hot warm meal every day for your future husband and kids. Give your husband the big piece of chicken because he's a king. Always pray with your husband and go fellowship at church with him. Please travel with him across the world! Have wild sex with him! Scream and shout with a lot of passion. Women build your husband up with kind words.

Remember, you know how lonely it is to be single. Doing a lot on your own! Open your heart like a baseball field! Trust like you never been hurt!

Sista, You're Taking Him For Granted

She just doesn't know I would fight a UFC fighter to meet and marry my future husband. To have someone who would to take l-o-n-g walks and talks with me. Someone who desire me and would make love to me all night long. Someone who would share my dreams and passion. Someone who would praise, worship and pray to God with me! Take my loneliness away! Someone who would go to amusement parks with me, go to concerts with me to listen and dance to live music, camping, hiking, snowboarding, riding bikes and enjoys listening to old school music like the 70's,80's and 90's Era. Oh, what a time we would have. Lord hear my S.O.S

His Each Stroke

Each stroke with love, each stroke with care, each stroke with passion, each with pleasure, each stroke with excitement, each stroke with JOY, each stroke was sensual, each stroke with laughter, each stroke with smiles, each stroke with purpose, each stroke with affection, each stroke with memories, each stroke unbreaking my heart, each stroke with vows, each stroke with protection, each stroke with safety, each stroke with direction, each stroke with prosperity and each stroke with God hands in the midst.